W9-CYS-432

Book Of Poems

Written and illustrated
BY

Eric C. Goose

Dedicated to everybody

All rights reserved
Copy write 2016

Dragon

My name is Hiromi
And I live in Japan
Every morning I wake
I love who I am

I will watch my T.V.
Then play with my Mommy
We can make many things
Like origami

I made a small dragon
And i hung it with strings
Was dancing around it
And the it grew wings

It was flying around
It flew up - ilt flew down
Then out of the window
And on to the ground

I did'nt believe it
Even with my own eyes
The strangest thing happend
And came by suprise

From now on I'll think twice
When all logic defies
I am now seeing why
They're called dragonflies

Go Kart

I am the king of my block
When it comes to the race
With go-karts we ride
At a very quick pace

Jamie's got lemonade
It is ten cents a glass
She makes it so great
That it's in its own class

Now I'm back in the chase
Not a hair out of place
Shirt is pressed neatly
There's a smile on my face

I'm in second place now
But I'm looking to pass
I'm sure I would win
If I weren't out of gas

Mister

DoYouHaveTheTime

"Excuse me son, did the bus go by?

I'm always running late.

I always have a place to go...

But never on a date.

Do you have the time young man?

My watch is on the fritz.

I always have a place to be

When not busy having fits.

My name is Doyouhavethetime,

And I must admit,...

I have a many place to go

But haven't made it to one yet.

Up-Side

Down

Which way is right side up
When I hang upside down
I am feeling whoosy
My smile is a frown

looking up I see green
I look down to see blue
Ahead a kid's laughing
And I think that it's you

I don't see what's funny
I'm not laughing at all
When I hang upside down
I don't feel so tall

I hear with my feet
And talk out of my ears
Sometimes It gets muffled
And nobody hears

I'm upside now down
Right up side and then
Backwards come my words
Upside down back again

Mix and Match

Mix and match a bunch or batch
Of unscratched unhatched eggs.
Mash and thrash potatoes
With a mismatched sawed off peg.
Stash the hash and bash your ladles.
Smash tomatoes too.
You don't know it... now you're making...
Really nasty stew.

Circles

and

Squares

What will fit into my circles and squares?
Will peaches, bananas, apples or pears?
I asked all my friends but nobody cares
How I will fill up my circles and squares.

Would a mulberry pie fit in the square?
I think that it would but I don't think you'd dare.
I have an idea and this one is rare.
I'll put you in the circle and me in the square.

A Pickin' My Fat Nose

I'm like a chicken cluckin'
I'm picking and I'm pluckin'
A plucking and a pickin'
A picking my fat nose

I see the ducks a duckin'
When hunters come a huntin'
They waddle waddle waddle
They waddle as they go

It seems the ducks have fun
Flying high up with the crows
I will stay here on the ground
Mud squishing through my toes

For now I'll keep a cluckin'
A picking and a pluckin'
A plucking and a pickin'
A picking my fat nose

Thank you for reading my book of poems.

Have you read my other books?

I know you will like them.

There is Brenda's Bubble

And...I asked The Animals
Well, I have to go write some more books now. Hope we meet again.

Made in the USA
Columbia, SC
31 May 2021

38528193R00015